SAVOUR
PRESS

turkish
recipes

A Turkish
Cookbook with
Kitchen Tested
Turkish Recipes

BEST TURKISH RECIPES

QUICK AND NUTRITIOUS TURKISH RECIPES

By
Savour Press
Copyright © by Wentworth Publishing House

Published by
Savour Press, a DBA of Wentworth Publishing House

Savour Press

Let's get it started!

Welcome to Savour. You might be wondering how foods are prepared in other places, and if this food tastes better than yours. If a foreign menu is served to you, would you eat it or ignore the chance of tasting without any obligations from you. There are times in our lives that we believe that our homegrown recipes are much better than others because we always love our own. *Savour* will tell you that whether the food comes from your country of origin or not, for as long as they are cooked with the right combination of spices, herbs, seasonings and blended with their local ingredients, and it is prepared with all your heart, the food taste delicious. When cooking, put your best foot forward with passion and dedication; the food is surely satisfying and delicious. This is the reason why we come up with another edition of our cookbook that though they are unfamiliar to you, will suit to your impeccable taste buds.

About This Book

Have you tried eating Turkish dish? Most probably you say yes, as kebabs are getting popular in restaurants and street foods. Kebabs are just one of the most famous Turkish recipes that come in a variety of shapes, color and flavors. In this edition, *Savour* proudly introduces to you the many facets of Turkish dishes via our 33 best Turkish main dishes and 10 best Turkish side dishes. They are properly selected for your satisfaction and underwent scrutiny. Amongst our dishes include Kavurma, Ali Nazik, Içli Köfte, Çöp Şiş, Karides Güveç, Kuzu Tandır, and a lot more. The names of these recipes might be foreign to your ears, but their images may sound familiar to you. The ingredients common in Turkish recipes include bulgur, eggplants, okra; lamb meat, Turkish kashar cheese, rice, and the rest are found in all types of cuisines like onions, garlic, parsley, mint, oil, pepper, and among others. We bet you will like the dishes. Let's get ready to have a fun time!

CONTENTS

INTRODUCTION

Turkish dishes are generally delightful, delicious and nutritious. Although their tastes and flavors are different from your homegrown dishes, their presentation is almost similar to some of your dishes, like kebabs, which is similar to your barbecued meats threaded on skewers. They love meatballs, which are usually a combination of bread crumbs from stale white bread, egg, flour, spices, herbs, lamb meat or beef meat or a combination of both. They also love eggplants, which are soaked in salty water to remove the bitter taste before roasting or grilling and are stuffed with lamb or beef meat mixture. These are only samples of what you will discover as you go through this book. Keep on reading.

Enjoy!

SIDE DISH
TURKISH BULGUR AND VEGETABLE PILAF

This hearty bulgur and veggie pilaf is economical and nutritious. Except for bulgur, all ingredients are easy to find or you already have it in your pantry. The bulgur is cooked with fried onion, tomato and green pepper with tomato paste, broth and seasoned with sugar, salt and pepper.

Servings: 4 servings (4 portions)

Ingredients

2 tablespoons **butter (margarine)**

2 tablespoons **olive oil** or **vegetable oil**

1 medium grated and well-drained **onion**

1 large grated **tomato with juice**

1 grated small **green pepper**

2 cups **coarse bulgur**

1/2 teaspoon **black pepper**

1 teaspoon **salt**

2 teaspoons **sugar**

2 tablespoons **tomato paste**

4 cups **chicken broth** or **water**

Garnish:

Fresh or grilled **pepper**

Chopped **tomato**

Fresh **Italian parsley**

Directions

Melt the butter and oil together in a covered shallow pan. Fry the grated onion for five minutes until tender and translucent.

Pour the grated tomato with juice and grated pepper; fry until the vegetables are soft and the liquid has almost gone.

Stir in the bulgur with a wooden spoon to combine well. Stir in the tomato paste, salt, pepper, broth and sugar and bring to a boil.

Cover and simmer on low heat for fifteen to twenty minutes until the cooking liquid is absorbed by the bulgur. Remove the pan from heat with cover, let cool.

Stir the pilaf just before serving until the ingredients are fully blended.

Serve in individual plate.

Garnish pilaf with grilled or fresh pepper, tomato slices, and parsley.

Enjoy!

Nutritional Information: 401 calorie; 12 g fat (2 g saturated fat); 0 mg cholesterol; 785 mg sodium; 67 g carbohydrate; 11 g dietary fiber; 13 g protein.

KISIR: TURKISH BULGUR SALAD

This popular Turkish salad has everything that makes your taste buds delighted. It is crunchy, soft, tangy and savory. While enjoying every bit of the mixed herbs and vegetables, you feel secure knowing they are all nutritious and great for entertaining your vegetarian guests.

Servings: 4-6 Portions (4-6 Servings)

Ingredients

2 cups **fine bulgur**

2 cups of **boiling water**

1 medium very finely chopped **onion**

1 very finely chopped **clove garlic**

1 heaping tablespoon **sweet red pepper paste**

2 very finely chopped medium **tomatoes**

2 very finely chopped medium **cucumbers**

6 to 8 very finely chopped **green onions**

Handful of very finely chopped **fresh Italian parsley leaves**

3 to 4 sprigs of very finely chopped **fresh mint**

1/4 cup of freshly squeezed **lemon juice** or **pomegranate sour**

1/3 cup **extra-virgin olive oil**

1/2 teaspoon **black pepper**

1 teaspoon **salt**

1/2 teaspoon **hot red pepper flakes**

DIRECTIONS:

Place bulgur in a large bowl and soak with enough boiling enough to cover. Cover the bowl with plastic wrap and wrap fully with a towel for fifteen minutes to soften the bulgur.

Prepare the vegetables by mixing the garlic and onion with pepper paste, set aside.

Place together in a separate bowl the tomato, green onions, cucumber, mint and parsley.

After fifteen minutes, remove the towel and plastic from the bowl of softened bulgur.

Fluff the bulgur up with your gloved fingers; drizzle with pomegranate sour or lemon juice and oil over the bulgur. Toss to coat well.

Add the pepper paste mixture to the bulgur and then mix them until coated.

Add the very finely chopped herbs and vegetables to the mixture.

Keep tossing with your gloved fingers until all flavors are blended. Sprinkle with black pepper and salt.

Now the kisir salad is ready to serve, or you can chill it for hours. Fluff up with your fingers before serving.

Enjoy!

Nutritional Information: 331 calorie; 13 g fat (2 g saturated fat); 0 mg cholesterol; 409 mg sodium; 50 g carbohydrate; 8 g dietary fiber; 8 g protein.

BULGUR & SUMMER VEGETABLE SALAD RECIPE

Summer is full of fun and adventure if you serve your family with this refreshing Turkish salad. It uses bulgur with diced cooked squash, tomatoes, zucchini, tomatoes, and flavored with lemon and olive oil. It is best served with barbecue or grilled fish.

Servings: 8

Ingredients

1 1/2 cups **fine bulgur**

2 teaspoon **salt**

4 cups **water**

2 tablespoon **olive oil**

1 diced **yellow summer squash**

1 diced **zucchini** or **courgette squash**

2 cups ripe **cherry tomatoes/ mini heirloom tomatoes**, cut into halves

1 bunch **fresh basil leaves**, pinch off the stems

1 teaspoon **salt**

1/3 cup **olive oil**

Juice of 1 lemon

Directions

Place the bulgur, salt and water in a large saucepan and bring to a boil.

Simmer with cover on low heat until the water has reduced. Turn off stove heat and let the bulgur steam and cool in saucepan.

Heat the olive oil in a skillet.

Sauté the squash and stir for a few minutes until slightly soft; set aside.

Use your fingers or wooden ladle to separate the grains when the bulgur is cool. Season the bulgur with salt, and toss to coat.

Pour the olive oil and lemon juice, work it through using your fingers until the bulgur is coated with oil.

Add the tomatoes, squash, and basil to the mixture and toss to coat thoroughly.

Serve!

Nutritional Information: 222 calorie; 13 g fat (2 g saturated fat); 0 mg cholesterol; 885 mg sodium; 25 g carbohydrate; 5 g dietary fiber; 5 g protein.

Turkish Okra And Tomato With Olive Oil

Fresh okra requires several washings and rinsing before and after soaking with vinegar. If you are using frozen ones, go directly to the next steps. While munching this zesty salad, there is no single trace of slime, and each bite is really awesome.

Servings: 8

Ingredients

2 1/2 pounds **fresh** or **frozen okra**

Juice of 1/2 lemon

1 coarsely chopped large **onion**

2 tablespoons of **olive oil**

1 large peeled and cubed ripe **tomato**

3 tablespoons **sugar**

1/2 teaspoon **black pepper**

3 teaspoons **salt**

1/3 cup **extra virgin olive oil**

Directions

Prepare fresh okra by trimming the rough stems from the tip of the pods. Remove and discard the thin membrane that covers the end of stems.

Wash the okra several times in a colander under ice cold water. Drain and soak in 1 cup vinegar for half an hour. Wash again to remove the vinegar and repeat once.

If you are using frozen okra, use it without doing this process.

Heat in a medium saucepan, two tablespoons of olive oil and sauté the onions until fragrant and tender. Stir-fry the okra and tomatoes.

Stir in lemon juice, sugar, salt and pepper and slowly turn with a wooden spoon. Pour the water and bring okra to a boil. Cover and gently simmer the okra until very tender and the water has almost evaporated.

Turn off heat and let the saucepan cool down. Pour the okra into a serving platter.

Garnish with 1/3 cup olive oil. Serve immediately or serve cold.

Enjoy!

Nutritional Information: 180 calorie; 13 g fat (2 g saturated fat); 0 mg cholesterol; 884 mg sodium; 16 g carbohydrate; 5 g dietary fiber; 3 g protein.

Turkish Roasted Eggplant Salad

Eggplants are versatile in the like that you can prepare it as a side dish. After extracting the flesh of eggplant, combine it with the rest of the ingredients and whip with a fork. You may add the optional ingredients for added flavor.

Servings: 8

Ingredients

3 or 4 large **globe eggplants**

4 to 5 tablespoons **extra virgin olive oil**

Pinch **Salt**

Dash **pepper**

Optional:

1 or 2 crushed **garlic cloves**

1 tablespoon **Greek yogurt** or **mayonnaise**

Directions

Heat up the grill and roast the eggplants.

Extract the flesh of the eggplant; remove and discard the skin and seeds of eggplant.

Place the flesh into a fine mesh strainer, squeezing out excess water and transfer to a large mixing bowl.

Add the salt, olive oil, pepper and crush garlic, if you desire.

Whip the mixture with a fork until fluffy and light.

When done, you may add the optional Greek yogurt or mayonnaise if you desire.

Refrigerate for thirty minute longer before serving.

Serve!

Nutritional Information: 111 calorie; 8 g fat (1 g saturated fat); 0 mg cholesterol; 43 mg sodium; 10 g carbohydrate; 2 g dietary fiber; 2 g protein.

CELERIAC COOKED TURKISH-STYLE MAKES A FRAGRANT VEGETABLE SIDE DISH

If you don't mind, celeriac belongs to the celery family and it makes every dish delicious. Though preparing the celeriac is a bit labor and time intensive, the result is really worth your effort. It is tangy, crunchy and sweet.

Servings: 4

Ingredients

2 large **celeriac** or **(kereviz)**

1 peeled large **carrot**, cut into 1/4-inch thick

1 quartered and coarsely sliced **small onion**, separate into rings

Juice of 1/2 lemon

Juice of 1 orange

1 teaspoon **sugar**

1/4 teaspoon **black pepper**

1 teaspoon **salt**

1/2 cup **extra-virgin olive oil**

Directions

Prepare the celeriac by cutting the stalks and sort them out. Save the fresh and green stalks and leaves; coarsely chop the leaves and green stalks, set aside. Peel the celeriac with a sharp knife, and cut into halves, about ½-inch thick.

Prepare a large covered saucepan and line the bottom with the celeriac slices.

Drizzle over the celeriac the orange and lemon juices to maintain their fresh look.

Arrange the carrots over the celeriac. Arrange onion slices over carrots.

Place the reserved coarsely chopped leaves and green stalks of celeriac.

Add ¼ cup olive oil, sugar, salt and pepper to the saucepan.

Pour ½ cup of water over the mixture and bring to a boil on high heat. Cover the pan and simmer the vegetable on low heat until tender and the liquid has reduced.

Remove the lid of saucepan if there is too much water, to quickly evaporate the liquid.

Turn off heat and let the veggies cool down in the saucepan.

Pour the vegetables into a serving plate; drizzle with ¼ cup of olive oil.

Garnish with chopped celery leaves.

Serve!

Nutritional Information: 278 calorie; 27 g fat (4 g saturated fat); 0 mg cholesterol; 644 mg sodium; 9 g carbohydrate; 2 g dietary fiber; 1 g protein.

HOME-STYLE TURKISH 'POĞAÇA'

This favorite Turkish breakfast menu will make your day bright and fruitful. The soft texture and the cheesy filling are really fantastic. Omit the parsley in the filling if you are using fresh herbs, and if using the herbs, add them to the dough.

Servings: 20 Rolls

Ingredients

1/3 cup crumbled **Feta** or **goat cheese**

2 cups **flour**

2 cups **plain yogurt**

3/4 cup melted **butter** or **margarine**

1/2 teaspoon **salt**

2 1/2 teaspoon **baking powder**

1/4 teaspoon **sugar**

2 **egg yolks**

2 tablespoons **sesame seeds** or **poppy seeds /black cumin seeds**

Optional:

1 tablespoon finely chopped **fresh parsley**

1/4 cup finely chopped **fresh herbs**

Directions

Prepare the filling by combining in a large bowl the crumbled feta cheese and 1 tablespoon parsley. If using herbs, omit parsley.

In another large bowl, combine two cups of flour and the rest of the ingredients. Mix and knead the mixture and slowly add the

27

remaining flour until the dough becomes smooth and firm. If using herbs, add them to the dough and knead.

Shape the dough into rolls of the size of your choice. You can have the size similar to a small plum or apricot.

Press the dough lightly on a work surface lightly dusted with flour. Place in the center of the flat dough with a filling of your choice, folding the circle in half on top of filling. Pinch to seal.

Place the poğaça or dough in a grease-proof baking paper lined-baking tray. Arrange the poğaça, seam side facing down and tuck its ends under.

Repeat the rest of the oval-shaped rolls (wide and round in the center and the ends are narrow). See to it that the rolls are one each apart.

Brush with egg yolk using a pastry brush. Sprinkle on top with poppy seeds, or sesame seeds or cumin seeds.

Bake at 350 degrees F until the surface is golden brown and the rolls puff up.

Serve with your favorite bread spread.

Enjoy!

Nutritional Information: 90 calorie; 7 g fat (2 g saturated fat); 26 mg cholesterol; 286 mg sodium; 5 g carbohydrate; 0 g dietary fiber; 3 g protein.

TURKISH BEANS: PINTO BEANS IN OLIVE OIL

This side dish is enough to make your stomach full with its heavy loads of pinto beans sautéed in olive oil along with tomatoes, carrots, spices and seasonings. If you are not using 2 ½ pounds of fresh pinto beans in their hulls, you can substitute it with 1 pound of hulled fresh pinto beans.

Servings: 8-10

Ingredients

3 tablespoons **extra virgin olive oil**

1 finely diced large **onion**

3 to 4 large diced **cloves garlic**

2 1/2 pounds **fresh pinto beans in their hulls**

1 large **carrot**, peeled and diced into small cubes

1 cup grated **tomatoes**

3 rounded tablespoons **tomato paste**

1/2 teaspoon **black pepper**

2 tablespoons **sugar**

2 teaspoons **salt**

1/3 cup **extra-virgin olive oil**

Chopped **Italian parsley**

Directions

Heat the 3 tablespoons olive oil in a covered saucepan and sauté the onion and garlic until fragrant and soft.

Stir in beans, grated tomato, carrots, tomato paste, sugar, pepper, and salt.

Add water to the mixture, just enough to cover the pinto beans. Stir and bring to a boil.

Cover and bring to a simmer on low heat until the liquid has reduced and the vegetables are tender-crisp. Turn off the heat and let the pan cool naturally.

Spoon the beans into individual bowls and drizzle on top with olive oil. Cover the bowl with cling wrap and refrigerate.

When ready to serve, sprinkle with Italian parsley leaves.

Enjoy!

Nutritional Information: 535 calorie; 13 g fat (2 g saturated fat); 0 mg cholesterol; 495 mg sodium; 82 g carbohydrate; 23 g dietary fiber; 26 g protein.

BOREK: LAYERED CHEESE PIE

This layered pie is known in Turkey as Borek, consisting of yufka with several fillings of milk mixture, cheese mixture and yufka sheets. As a favorite staple in Turkish cuisine, almost every family knows how to prepare it. The cheese used in this recipe is Turkish white cheese, feta or goat cheese.

Servings: 12

Ingredients

1 stick **butter** or **margarine** about 125 grams

4 cups **milk**

1 teaspoon **salt**

1/2 teaspoon **black pepper** or **white pepper**

6 large **yufka sheets**

4 **eggs**

4 tablespoons chopped **Italian parsley**

18 ounces crumbled **Turkish white cheese** or r**educed salt**

Feta/crumbly goat cheese

For garnish:

Sesame seeds or **nigella seeds**

Directions

Place the butter in a heat-proof bowl and melt in the microwave.

Stir in milk, pepper and salt and then microwave on high until the milk is warmed thoroughly, making sure not to scald.

Toss in another bowl the chopped parsley, egg and crumble white cheese.

Coat the bottom and sides of a large heat-proof baking tray with butter.

Drizzle on the bottom of tray with one or two tablespoons of milk mixture.

Cover the bottom of the tray with the first sheet of yufka by placing it unevenly. Fill the top of the wrinkled yufka sheet with one-sixth of the milk mixture, allowing it to spread to the edges and cracks of yufka.

Divide the cheese mixture into 5 equal parts and sprinkle 1/5 of it on top of yufka. Repeat the steps for the next yufka layer until you finish five yufka layers.

Cover the last pastry layer with yufka sheet.

Spread the remaining milk mixture on top to wet all over.

Sprinkle the surface with nigella seeds or sesame seeds.

Bake at 185 degrees F for forty-five minutes until the center firms up and the surface is nicely golden brown.

Remove from oven and sprinkle the top of the pastry with 1 to 2 tablespoons of cold water. Wrap with clean towel to soften the topmost layer.

Let stand for 20 minutes. Slice into squares.

Serve!

Nutritional Information: 405 calorie; 29 g fat (18 g saturated fat); 156 mg cholesterol; 679 mg sodium; 28 g carbohydrate; 0 g dietary fiber; 11 g protein.

TURKISH MELTED CHEESE AND CORNMEAL (MIHLAMA)

Mihlama is a popular Turkish breakfast staple that is cooked in a copper sahan or your typical frying pan. The creamy taste suits to your taste buds even if it is your first time to taste it. The secret is the blend of Trabzon village cheese, cornmeal and butter. You can also use Kashar or Turkish string cheese.

Servings: 4

Ingredients

6 tablespoons **unsalted butter**

6 tablespoons **cornmeal**

1 cup of **water**

10 ounces grated **Trabzon village cheese** or **Kashar cheese** or

Turkish string cheese

Directions

Melt the butter in a copper sahan (frying pan) for a few minutes until bubbly, but not burned.

Stir in the cornmeal, cook and stir with a large wooden spoon until the color turns into deep golden brown.

Add water to the mixture when the oil separates from the butter; bring water to a full boil.

Slowly add the cheese to the mixture, stirring often, until the cheese melts and the mixture is incorporated and smooth.

Simmer on low flame; stir until the butter is on top of the mixture. Remove from heat.

Serve immediately with bread.

Enjoy!

Nutritional Information: 458 calorie; 39 g fat (24 g saturated fat); 112 mg cholesterol; 404 mg sodium; 11 g carbohydrate; 1 g dietary fiber; 18 g protein.

Main Dishes
Turkish Eggplant and Ground Beef Casserole Recipe

This delicious Moussaka or layered meat and eggplant casserole are something that you should not miss at least once in your lifetime. If you are not familiar with this dish commonly served in the eastern Mediterranean region, Turkey, Greece and Balkans, take a look at how it is prepared.

Servings: 8

Ingredients

5 **eggplants**

2 cups **vegetable oil** for frying

1 chopped **onion**

1 tablespoon **olive oil**

1 **Hungarian pepper** or other **green, sweet pepper**

1 pound **lean ground beef**

1 large grated **tomato**

1 tablespoon **tomato paste**

1/2 teaspoon **black pepper**

1/2 teaspoon **allspice**

1 teaspoon **salt**

1 tablespoon **tomato paste**

3 grated large **tomatoes**

1/2 teaspoon **salt**

1/4 teaspoon **black pepper**

1/2 teaspoon **sugar**

1/2 teaspoon **oregano**

3 tablespoon **butter** or **margarine**

3 tablespoon **flour**

3 cups of **milk**

1 cup grated **Turkish kaşar**, or **yellow cheese**

Garnish:

Sweet red pepper strips

Slices **green pepper**

Directions

Peel the eggplants using a peeler starting at the end. Remove a strip of skin from end to end, leaving a strip of skin of the same width and then peel another strip of skin from end to end to resemble a stripe pattern.

Repeat this step for the rest of the eggplant, and then slice them about ¼ inches thick.

Place the eggplant slices in a large mixing bowl with salty water and soak for half an hour to remove the bitter taste.

Prepare the green pepper by slicing into rings.

Heat in a large frying pan the 1 tablespoon of olive oil and sauté the onion until tender. Add the green pepper rings and sauté until soft. Add the ground beef to the mixture, sauté until browned.

Pour the tomato paste, spices and grated tomato. Stir and cover the pan, bring to a simmer for ten minutes. Remove pan from heat.

Place the three grated tomatoes in a small saucepan and add the tomato paste, oregano, sugar, salt and pepper. Bring to a simmer for ten minutes and remove from heat.

Drain the eggplant slices and blot dry with paper towels.

Heat 2 cups of vegetable oil and fry the dried eggplant slices until both sides are golden brown and tender. Drain excess oil on paper towels.

Place the fried eggplant on the bottom of a large baking tray to form a single layer, no gaps in between.

Evenly spread the tomato sauce over the fried eggplants.

Evenly spread the meat mixture over the tomato sauce layer. Set aside.

Melt in a large pan the butter on high heat, adding the flour and turn with wooden spoon.

Pour the milk and seasonings, while whisking until the béchamel sauce is smooth and thick, similar to the pudding consistency.

Evenly spread the hot béchamel sauce all over the meat layer and evenly cover the béchamel sauce with grated cheese.

Bake at 360 degrees F until the surface of casserole becomes golden brown. Remove from oven and let stand for ten minutes.

Cut casserole into squares.

Serve with Turkish-style rice pilaf.

Enjoy!

Nutritional Information: 941 calorie; 76 g fat (12 g saturated fat); 75 mg cholesterol; 405 mg sodium; 41 g carbohydrate; 13 g dietary fiber; 28 g protein.

TURKISH MENEMEN VEGETABLE AND EGG SCRAMBLE

You will truly love this Turkish breakfast dish if you love egg omelet. The vegetables are sautéed in butter and cooked in a gentle simmer, and then the scrambled eggs are poured into the vegetable mixture without stirring until cooked. For added flavor, add extra butter to the menemen before serving.

Servings: 1 menemen (serves 2)

Ingredients

4 tablespoon **butter**

1 finely chopped large **onion**

2 large diced ripe **tomatoes**

2 **sweet red peppers**

2 **sweet green peppers** or 1 **hot chili pepper**

1 teaspoon **salt**

1/2 teaspoon **black pepper**

6 **eggs**

Optional:

1 teaspoon **hot red pepper flakes**

Directions

Remove skin of tomatoes and cut into dice, reserve the juice. Remove seeds of peppers and cut into dice.

Melt 4 tablespoons of butter in a large pan and sauté the onion until transparent and tender.

Add the diced tomatoes, diced peppers, salt and black pepper. Stir to combine well and bring to a boil.

Cover and simmer on low heat until the vegetables are softened and their juices release naturally. Remove cover and gently simmer until the liquid has nearly evaporated.

Scramble the eggs in a bowl and sprinkle with salt. Pour the egg into the center of the vegetable mixture.

Avoid stirring the mixture until the eggs scatter throughout the vegetables naturally. Cook until the eggs are set and cooked. Cover the pan if the eggs are still raw.

Remove menemen from heat when fully cooked, but still juicy.

Drizzle extra melted butter on top of menemen if desired.

Serve!

Nutritional Information: 557 calorie; 40 g fat (20 g saturated fat); 686 mg cholesterol; 1423 mg sodium; 26 g carbohydrate; 7 g dietary fiber; 25 g protein.

TURKISH RICE PILAF WITH CHICKEN AND CHICK PEAS

This one dish meal is enough to recharge your body as it is complete with vegetables, rice and chicken. Each serving of rice pilaf is fulfilling, especially if you serve it with Turkish yogurt drink or cold ayran. It is perfect for lunchtime, dinner or potluck.

Servings: 4

Ingredients

1/2 **whole chicken with skin**

1 peeled **onion**

1 peeled **carrot**

1 (12 ounces) can drained and rinsed **chickpeas**

2 tablespoons **olive oil**

2 tablespoons **butter**

2 cups **chicken broth**

1 1/2 cup **short grain rice**

2 teaspoons **salt**

1/2 teaspoon **black pepper**

1 cup **water**

Directions

Put the chicken in a large pot filled with enough water to cover by 1 inch.

Place the peeled onion and carrots in the pot and bring to a boil. Cover the pot and gently simmer on low heat for thirty minutes until the meat falls off the bones.

Turn off heat and set aside to cool. Discard the carrot and onion when the meat has cooled off.

Remove the chicken from the liquid, separating the meat from the bones and discard the skin, gristle and bones.

Using a fine wire strainer, strain the broth and set aside.

Melt the butter and oil in a large and shallow pan.

Stir in the rice until coated with the melted butter and oil using a wooden spoon. Continue frying the dry rice on low heat for a few minutes.

Stir in the chick peas and add the water, spices and chicken broth; bring to a boil. Simmer on low heat and cover until the liquid is absorbed by the rice. Turn off heat and open the top of the pan.

Neatly arrange the chicken over the cooked rice the soonest possible to prevent losing the steam.

Replace the cover of the pan and continue steaming the rice for ten minutes longer. Remove the lid when it is about time to serve the pilaf.

Place the chicken pieces in the bottom and up to the sides of a large bowl.

Fill the bowl with hot rice using a wooden spoon and pack it gently to make the pilaf firm.

When fully packed, turn the bowl upside down on each serving plate and garnish the top with chopped fresh herbs.

Serve immediately with a glass of cold ayran or Turkish yogurt drink.

Enjoy!

Nutritional Information: 756 calorie; 25 g fat (8 fat saturated fat); 68 mg cholesterol; 1726 mg sodium; 97 g carbohydrate; 10 g dietary fiber; 34 g protein.

TURKISH SPICY MEATLESS "STEAK" TARTAR (ÇIĞ KÖFTE) RECIPE

This meatless steak tartar aka çiğ Köfte is loaded with pureed tomatoes, onions, cloves, bulgur, and walnut halves. It is blended with spices, tomato paste, isot biber, pomegranate concentrate and red pepper paste and kneaded, and then placed overnight in a tightly covered bowl and serve the following day.

Servings: 6

Ingredients

2 cups **fine bulgur**

5 large **ripe tomatoes**

2 peeled & coarsely chopped medium **onions**

5 peeled & coarsely chopped **garlic cloves**

1 cup **walnut halves**

2 slices **stale bread**

1/2 cup **pomegranate concentrate**

1/2 cup **olive oil**

1 tablespoon **tomato paste**

1/4 cup of **Turkish isot biber**

1 teaspoon **cumin**

1 teaspoon **salt**

1 tablespoon **red pepper paste**

Garnish:

Finely chopped **fresh parsley & green onion**

For serving:

Romaine lettuce leaves

Sliced **lemon**

Directions

Wash and peel the tomatoes and place in a food processor. Pulse until it becomes smooth.

In place of a food processor, use a hand grater and finely grate the tomatoes.

Wash the bulgur under cold running water directly in a wire strainer until the water runs clear.

Drain and place in large mixing bowl together with the tomato puree, mixing until incorporated. Cover and let stand for 1 hour until the bulgur is soft.

Put the coarsely chopped garlic and onions in a food processor with the walnut halves and stale bread.

Process at high speed until it becomes a fine powder. Pour into the bulgur and tomato mixture.

Add the rest of the ingredients and knead with your gloved hands until incorporated.

Divide into small portions to accommodate in the food processor and process in batches at medium speed until it becomes smooth.

Mix all pureed mixture in a large mixing bowl and knead until it becomes thick.

Put the mixture in a bowl and tightly cover. Let stand for five hours or overnight.

When ready to use, break off the bite-sized pieces and form them into fingerprint shapes.

Arrange the Çiğ Köfte on a serving plate with fresh lemon slivers and romaine lettuce leaves.

Enjoy!

Nutritional Information: 571 calorie; 33 g fat (4 g saturated fat); 0 mg cholesterol; 508 mg sodium; 64 g carbohydrate; 12 g dietary fiber; 13 g protein.

Turkish Shrimp And Vegetable Clay Pot Casserole 'Karides Güveç'

This show stopping karides güveç or clay pot casserole is simple to do, yet its taste is magnificent. This is a real appetizer with its creamy goodness brought by the melted Turkish fresh kashar cheese and the blend of ingredients that are absorbed by the shrimp. The extra juice is great for dipping your crusty bread.

Servings: 4

Ingredients

1 pound frozen or fresh **uncooked shrimp**

2 to 3 peeled and diced **cloves garlic**

1 peeled and diced **onion**

3 tablespoons **olive oil**

2 to 3 ripe peeled and diced **tomatoes**

2 to 3 **Hungarian wax peppers** or 1 to 2 **green bell peppers**

¼ teaspoon **black pepper**

1 cup small fresh or canned **button mushrooms**

1 teaspoon **salt**

1 tablespoon **tomato paste**

¼ teaspoon **hot red pepper flakes** (optional)

1 cup grated **Turkish fresh kashar cheese** or other **mild & yellow cheese**

Directions

Fill a medium pot with water and 1 teaspoon of salt; bring to a boil.

Place the shrimp in boiling water for 1 to 2 minutes.

Drain in a colander and rinse the shrimp under cold running water to prevent overcooking.

Remove seeds of green peppers, and dice the same size with tomatoes.

Wash the mushrooms.

Heat olive oil in a large saucepan and sauté the garlic and onions until translucent and soft.

Stir-fry the green peppers and then the diced tomato. Add the mushrooms, spices and tomato paste and simmer until the cooking liquid is almost evaporated.

Stir in cooked shrimp and turn gently with a wooden spoon to coat the shrimp.

Pour the mixture into an oven-proof dishes or small clay pots.

Spread a generous amount of grated cheese on top.

Place the casserole in the oven on the oven rack. Cook on broil setting until the cheese becomes bubbly and nicely browned. Remove from oven.

Serve piping hot with crusty bread.

Serve!

Nutritional Information: 476 calorie; 22 g fat (8 g saturated fat); 258 mg cholesterol; 807 mg sodium; 33 g carbohydrate; 6 g dietary fiber; 40 g protein.

TURKISH-STYLE LAMB 'KAVURMA'

Probably this recipe is the easiest and simplest ever created when it comes to preparing lamb. You only need three ingredients with salt as your seasoning. Cook the lamb with salt in a saucepan for several hours until the liquid has dried out and the meat falls apart.

Servings: 4 to 6

Ingredients

¼ pound **lamb** or **tail fat**

2 to 3 pounds **boneless lamb roast** or **boneless leg and thigh of lamb**

2 teaspoons **salt**

Directions

Use a sharp knife when you are using a leg lamb with bone. Slice the lamb meat off its bones in large chunks. Remove unwanted parts and leave the soft part and fat. The bone can be used for preparing the broth for future use.

If using a boneless lamb roast, just cut the fat and meat into bite-sized cubes.

Place the meat cubes in a saucepan and season with salt using your bare hands.

Start cooking on high heat until the bottom of pan sizzles. Cover the saucepan and simmer the meat on low heat, and then gently simmer for a couple of hours.

Make sure to turn the meat from time to time using a large wooden spoon.

The meat will be ready when it falls apart, the color is dark and the liquid is gone, with fats left in the pan.

Now it's time to serve the kavurma with bulgur or rice pilaf.

Serve!

Nutritional Information: 577 calorie; 40 g fat (17 g saturated fat); 195 mg cholesterol; 934 mg sodium; 0 g carbohydrate; 0 g dietary fiber; 51 g protein.

TURKISH BAKED EGGPLANT FILLED WITH GROUND BEEF

Every Turkish household loves to prepare this karnıyarık or fried eggplant stuffed with sautéed browned beef, onions, garlic and tomatoes and baked until crusty. For better results, choose young eggplant; soak it with salted water, drain and fry.

Servings: 12

Ingredients

3 pounds **Japanese eggplant** or **oblong eggplant**

2 cups **vegetable oil** for frying

4 tablespoons **olive oil**

3 crushed **onions**

3 **green bell peppers**

7 ripe **tomatoes**

3 tablespoons **tomato paste**

½ teaspoon **black pepper**

1 1/2 pounds **ground beef**

2 teaspoons **salt**

2 finely chopped **cloves garlic**

½ teaspoon **red pepper flakes**

1 cup chopped **Italian parsley leaves**

Directions

Create a stripe pattern when preparing the eggplant by peeling into alternate stripe from end to end using a sharp knife or vegetable peeler.

Soak the eggplants in salted water and leave it there while preparing the other ingredients.

Heat the olive oil in a large pan and fry the onions until tender and shrunk.

Sauté the ground beef until browned.

Peel with a sharp paring knife 5 pieces of tomatoes; dice into cubes. Add the tomatoes to the pan and stir until soft. Drain excess tomato juice if using canned and diced tomatoes before adding to the meat.

Add the garlic and spices to the mixture, and stir frequently. Stir in chopped parsley and continue stirring for three minutes. Turn off heat and let the mixture stand for a few minutes.

Remove the eggplants from the soaking liquid, drain and blot dry with paper towels.

Heat in another pan the vegetable oil. Fry the whole eggplants and turn the other side to cook evenly. When softened, remove the eggplants from oil and drain on paper towels.

Neatly line up the eggplants in an oven-proof baking dish side by side.

With a paring knife, gently open up each eggplant by cutting a slit from end to end. Fill each fried eggplant with equal amount of meat mixture.

Slice the remaining two tomatoes thinly and into halve. Place the tomatoes slices on top of meat filling. Repeat the same procedure for the peppers.

In a small bowl, stir the tomato paste in water and pour into the dish.

Cook the eggplant for half an hour at 375 degrees F. Remove dish from oven and let stand for a few minutes.

Serve!

Nutritional Information: 593 calorie; 49 g fat (6 g saturated fat); 50 mg cholesterol; 458 mg sodium; 22 g carbohydrate; 7 g dietary fiber; 20 g protein.

Turkish Tripe Soup

This recipe is meticulously prepared from beginning to end. The tripe is washed many times and bleached with baking soda solution before cooking for 4 hours at a gentle simmer with spices and then thickened with egg yolks, flour and butter. Each bowl of soup is served with crushed garlic and vinegar.

Servings: 4-6

Ingredients

1 pound dressed **veal tripe**

12 cups of **water**

1 tablespoon **salt**

2 tablespoons **butter** or **margarine**

2 to 3 **meat bouillon cubes**

1 tablespoon **flour**

Juice of 1 lemon

2 **egg yolks**

4 crushed **cloves garlic**

1 cup **vinegar**

3 tablespoons **butter** or **margarine**

1 tablespoon **hot red pepper flakes**

Directions

Remove the membrane and fat of tripe. Wash and bleach in baking soda solution to evenly whiten its color.

In a large pot, boil the water and add salt. Add the tripe to the pot, cover and simmer for four hours.

While cooking the tripe, make sure to remove the scum that floats in the sides and surface of cooking liquid.

Remove tripe from the broth when tender. Cut the tripe into thin bite-sized pieces and return to the broth. Stir in the bouillon cubes and bring to a gentle simmer.

Melt in a pan the margarine or butter and stir in flour until lightly brown.

Slowly whisk with a few ladleful of hot soup to the pot until the mixture is consistent; pour into the soup when it becomes thick and smooth. Gently simmer the soup for 15 minutes.

Meanwhile, beat the eggs with lemon juice in a small bowl and slowly whisking into the soup. Stir often and bring to scalding point, but not boiling. Turn off stove.

In another pan, melt the margarine or butter, stirring in hot pepper flakes.

Sprinkle a teaspoonful of butter mixture on top of individual bowl of soup.

Combine crushed garlic and vinegar in a bowl and spoon into soup when serving.

Serve!

Nutritional Information: 877 calorie; 39 g fat (14 g saturated fat); 234 mg cholesterol; 1577 mg sodium; 74 g carbohydrate; 10 g dietary fiber; 59 g protein.

TURKISH-STYLE CREAM OF TOMATO SOUP RECIPE

This Turkish version of tomato soup is best served before lunchtime or dinner. You often see Turkish people snacking with this savory soup and dipped with crusty bread. The soup is a blend of butter, tomato juice, whole milk and topped with Turkish kashar cheese

Servings: 4

Ingredients

3 tablespoons **butter** or **margarine**

2 tablespoons **flour**

1/4 teaspoon **black pepper**

2 teaspoons **salt**

4 cups of **tomato juice**

1 cup **whole milk**

1/2 cup grated **Turkish kashar cheese** or **mozzarella**

Directions

Melt in a covered saucepan the butter or margarine.

Stir in the flour until bubbly, but not darkened or burned.

Gradually add the tomato juice, whisking or stirring often with a wire whisk and bring to a gentle boil.

Season the mixture with salt and pepper, stirring to combine. Cover and gently simmer for ten minutes.

Remove the lid and pour the milk, stirring frequently, until steaming and warmed through, but not boiling. If the mixture still not consistent, add more milk and stir often.

When it reaches the desired consistency, ladle the soup into individual bowls.

Garnish with grated cheese. Serve with crunchy bread.

Enjoy!

Nutritional Information: 256 calorie; 13 g fat (4 g saturated fat); 15 mg cholesterol; 1703 mg sodium; 28 g carbohydrate; 3 g dietary fiber; 8 g protein.

MEAT CUPS FILLED WITH MASHED POTATOES RECIPE

These 'Çanak Köftesi' or meat cups are guaranteed to tickle your taste buds. By the looks of it, you know it is suitable to non-Turkish diners. The meat cup is stuffed with mashed potatoes and topped with grated Turkish kashar before cooking in the oven.

Servings: 4 to 6

Ingredients

For the meat mixture:

1 pound **ground beef (10 or 20% fat content)**

1 teaspoon **salt**

1 **egg**

½ teaspoon **black pepper**

1 teaspoon **garlic powder**

1 teaspoon **onion powder**

1 teaspoon **paprika**

1 teaspoon **cumin**

¼ cup finely chopped **fresh Italian parsley**

4 slices **stale white sandwich bread**

For the potato filling:

1 pound **potatoes**

2 tablespoon **butter** or **margarine**

½ teaspoon **ground white pepper**

1 teaspoon **salt**

1/3 cup **milk**

For the topping:

1/3 cup **grated Turkish kashar** or other **mild cheese**

Directions

Prepare the meat cups by mixing in a bowl with the ground beef, egg, salt, black pepper, onion powder, garlic powder, cumin, Italian parsley, and paprika.

Slowly remove the crusts from the bread and sprinkle with water until wet, and squeeze out excess liquid. Mix the wet bread to the ground beef mixture.

Knead the ingredients with your gloved hands until the mixture becomes stiffened and thickened like dough. Cover with plastic wrap and let stand for fifteen minutes.

Tear apart a ball of the meat mixture and create a hole in the middle using your finger. Lengthen the sides of "dough" going upwards and then enlarge the hole with your fingers similar when shaping pottery.

Place the meat cup on a baking tray and do the rest of the meat mixture until the entire tray is fully filled.

Peel the potatoes and boil until very soft. Drain and mash the potatoes with a hand masher while still hot. Stir in the butter, salt and ground white pepper and mash again until incorporated.

Using an electric mixer beat the mashed ingredients for several minutes until no longer lumpy. Stir in milk while beating until soft peaks are formed.

Fill the center of meat cups with equal amount of the mashed potato, piling high to create a mountain peak on top of the meat cup. Sprinkle each peak with grated cheese.

Bake at 390 degrees F until the meatballs are fully cooked and the peaks are slightly browned for twenty minutes.

Serve the çanak köftesi' immediately with salad or pilaf.

Serve!

Nutritional Information: 352 calorie; 17 g fat (8 g saturated; 123 mg cholesterol; 969 mg sodium; 21 g carbohydrate; 2 g dietary fiber; 28 g protein.

Turkish Roasted Lamb (Kuzu Tandir)

This roasted lamb or Kuzu tandır has been always part of every Turkish celebration. Each lamb piece is super tender-juicy after roasted in the oven for several hours. The tangy flesh easily falls off from the bone, making it palatable even for the elderly.

Servings: 1 Leg of Lamb (8 Servings)

Ingredients

1 leg of **lamb (drumstick and thigh portions)**

1/2 teaspoon **black pepper**

1/4 cup **olive oil**

1 teaspoon **salt**

Juice of 1/2 lemon

2 to 3 **fresh rosemary sprigs**

4 to 5 **bay leaves**

1/2 cup **hot water**

Directions

Prepare the lamb leg by cleaning off excess fat and separate at the joints into three pieces.

Preheat the oven at 285 degrees F. Put the lamb in a shallow oven roasting tray.

Whisk in a bowl the lemon juice, olive oil, salt, and black pepper; pour over the lamb. Rub the lemon mixture all over the lamb, making sure to massage the meat several seconds.

Add the rosemary sprigs and bay leaves to the mixture.

After massaging the lamb, place in the oven without cover. Slowly cook the lamb for 1 ½ hours without adjusting the oven temperature.

Turn the lamb pieces after the first thirty minutes of cooking. Do this twice during cooking.

After 1 ½ hours of cooking and the meat has been turned thrice, pour a half cup of hot water all over the meat and cover the roasting pan with aluminum foil.

Roast the meat at 365 degrees F for 1 hour longer. After an hour, remove the roasting pan from the oven and let stand for five minutes. Discard the foil.

At this moment, the meat is very tender and easily falls off from the bones. Remove the flesh from the bones and discard the bones, bay leaves and rosemary.

Serve the kuzu tandır piping hot with orzo or rice pilaf.

Enjoy!

Nutritional Information: 162 calorie; 13 g fat (4 g saturated fat); 32 mg cholesterol; 28 mg sodium; 2 g carbohydrate; 1 g dietary fiber; 9 g protein.

Turkish Ezogelin Soup With Red Lentils, Bulgur, and Rice

This hearty and creamylicious ezogelin soup is satisfying with its nutritious blend of red lentils, bulgur, rice, pepper paste, onion and broth. The flour is fried until bubbly to add a consistent texture to the ezogelin, so there is no need to serve this with bread.

Servings: 4-6

Ingredients

4 tablespoons **butter** or **margarine**, divided

1 very finely chopped **onion**

1 heaping tablespoon **flour**

2 tablespoons **sweet red pepper paste** or **tomato paste**

1/2 cup large **grain rice**

1 1/2 cups **red lentils**

1/4 cup **coarse bulgur**

2 teaspoons **salt**

8 cups **beef broth** or **bouillon**

1 teaspoon **dried mint**

1 teaspoon **hot red pepper flakes**

Directions

Melt three tablespoons of the butter or margarine in a large and covered saucepan.

Fry the onion until tender and transparent.

Stir in flour until bubbly, but not browned or burned.

In a small bowl, stir in tomato paste or pepper in two tablespoons of water and pour into the flour, stirring to combine.

Slowly stir in the broth, stirring often on high heat until it brings to a boil.

Meanwhile, wash together the rice, bulgur and red lentils in a fine wire strainer under cold running water until the water is clear.

Pour the rice mixture to the boiling soup. Cover and reduce the stove heat.

Add bouillon to the soup and reduce the salt.

Bring the soup to a gentle simmer for twenty minutes, until the lentils are falling apart and the grains are very soft.

Melt in a small pan with the remaining 1 tablespoon of butter and add the mint and hot pepper flakes. Stir for 1 to 2 minutes, and then add to the soup.

Bring to a simmer for several minutes, adding a little broth or water if the soup is too thick.

Serve ezogelin in bowls.

Garnish with one lemon slice, or mint or red pepper flakes.

Serve!

Nutritional Information: 482 calorie; 15.2 g fat (8.2 g saturated fat); 31 mg cholesterol; 2824 mg sodium; 55.9 g carbohydrate; 23.2 g dietary fiber; 4.1 g total sugars; 29.5 g protein.

TURKISH MEATBALL AND POTATO CASSEROLE RECIPE

This extraordinary casserole is baked with perfection with its chilly flavor and saucy texture. It uses lots of sweet peppers, tomatoes and tomato paste and place on top of fried potatoes. The lowest bottom of the casserole lays the fried meatballs mixed with black pepper, cumin, egg, parsley and stale bread.

Servings: 6-8

Ingredients

2 cups **cooking oil**

1 pound **ground lean beef**

1 grated **onion**

4 slices **stale white bread**

1/4 chopped **Italian parsley leaves**

1 **egg**

1/2 teaspoon **cumin**

1/2 teaspoon **black pepper**

1 1/2 teaspoon **salt**

4 large peeled **potatoes** cut into wedges

1 **green bell pepper**

1 **red bell pepper**

3 to 4 **Hungarian peppers**

2 grated **tomatoes**

1 tablespoon **tomato paste**

1/2 teaspoon **salt**

1 cup **hot water**

Directions

Prepare the meatballs by putting the ground beef in a mixing bowl and add the grated onion.

Remove the crust of stale bread and wet with warm water, squeezing excess water out and add to the ground meat. Add the chopped parsley, egg, salt, black pepper and cumin.

Mix the ingredients together and knead for several minutes until incorporated. Let mixture rest for a few minutes.

Tear apart the walnut-sized pieces of the mixture and form into oblong-shaped meatballs by rolling between the palms of your hands.

Heat a generous amount of oil, enough to cover the meat, in a large pan on high heat.

Add the meatballs and fry until both sides are nicely browned. Drain fried meatballs on paper towel-lined plate.

Meanwhile, fry the wedged-cut potatoes in the leftover oil used in frying the meatballs until lightly golden brown and soft. Drain fried potatoes on paper towels.

Arrange in a large heat-proof casserole tray the fried meatballs until fully covered.

Arrange on top of meatballs an even layer of fried potatoes.

Wash 2 tomatoes and cut into wedges. Wash the red and green peppers, and cut into large strips. Arrange the tomato wedges and pepper strips together with the layer of potatoes.

Combine in a bowl the 2 grated tomatoes, hot water, tomato paste, salt and pepper and pour over the casserole.

Bake at 390 degrees F for thirty minutes until the vegetables are soft and slightly browned.

Serve the casserole with crusty bread.

Enjoy!

Nutritional Information: 711 calorie; 63 g fat (11 g saturated fat); 77 mg cholesterol; 673 mg sodium; 19 g carbohydrate; 3 g dietary fiber; 20 g protein.

New World (Loquat) Kebab

Add a twist to your barbecue by incorporating the Turkish method of grilling meat, called kebab with loquats. Since most Turkish kebabs are a bit spicy, this recipe is milder and taste so sweet, blending perfectly with the meat juices and bringing out the smoky flavor from the grill.

Servings: 8-10 Kebab (4 servings)

Ingredients

1 pound **ground beef (30% fat)**

1/4 cup chopped **Italian parsley**

1 teaspoon **black pepper**

2 teaspoons **salt**

45 pieces medium **loquats**

50 **fresh bay leaves**

8 to 10 long metal skewers for grill

Directions

Knead in a large bowl the ground beef, chopped parsley, salt and pepper for several times. Cover the bowl and let the mixture rest for several minutes.

Prepare the loquats by washing it and removing the stems. Cut in half from end to end. Slowly remove the pits and its inner membranes using your index finger.

Tear apart a portion of the meat mixture and roll out to form a small walnut-sized ball.

Press the meatball into loquat half and then cover with the other loquat half. Repeat with the rest of the meat mixture and loquats.

Thread the bay leaf onto a skewer and followed by 4 or 5 pieces of meat-stuffed loquats with bay leaf threaded between each other.

Grill the kebab on medium fire and turn the other side until done and well-browned.

Serve!

Nutritional Information: 161 calorie; 4 g fat (1.5 g saturated fat); 51 mg cholesterol; 622 mg sodium; 14 g carbohydrate; 2.7 g dietary fiber; 0 g total sugars; 18 g protein.

ALI NAZIK RECIPE

Ali Nazik exemplifies the real tender juicy lamb chunks placed over the warm fire-roasted eggplant with yogurt mixture. The topmost part is garnished with spicy pan juices, oil, melted butter, fire roasted pepper and tomato pieces. It is best served with pide or Turkish flat bread.

Servings: 4

Ingredients

For the Eggplant Mash:

4 medium **Japanese eggplants**

2 **cloves garlic**

1 cup **plain** or **Greek yogurt**

1/2 teaspoon **black pepper**

1 teaspoon **salt**

For the Meat Topping:

1 **tomato**

1/2 pound **lamb**

2 tablespoons **butter**

1 **sweet green pepper**

1 teaspoon **red pepper paste** or **tomato paste**

2 tablespoons **vegetable oil**

1/2 teaspoon **black pepper**

1 teaspoon **salt**

2 to 3 tablespoons **water**

Garnish:

Chopped **fresh parsley**

Directions

Wash the eggplants and pierce all over with a toothpick or a thin skewer.

Heat up a coal fire or gas grill and place the eggplants over it. Roast until the eggplants collapse and turn to cook the other side.

Wash the tomato and pepper and cut them into quarters. Grill them next to the eggplants, turning once, until both sides are browned.

Meanwhile, chop the lamb into bite-sized chunks as small as the kidney beans.

Melt in a skillet the 2 tablespoons butter and cook the lamb until tender and the juice are released naturally.

While cooking the lamb, add the pepper paste, pepper, salt and vegetable oil, covering the pan and simmer on low heat. Continue cooking the lamb on a gentle simmer until very tender, adding a few teaspoonful of water if needed.

While doing this, it is assumed that the eggplants are now soft, remove them from the grill, and then run a knife down its entire length and open up.

Scoop the flesh and mix with the plain or Greek yogurt with salt and pepper.

To serve the Ali nazik, cover the entire bottom of your serving platter with the warm eggplant and yogurt mixture. Place a spoonful of the meat mixture on top.

Drizzle with oil and pan juices on top. Add extra melted butter for extra flavor and garnish with the grilled tomato and pepper pieces.

Sprinkle with a pinch of chopped parsley.

Enjoy!

Nutritional Information: 299 calorie; 17.6 g fat (7.1 g saturated fat); 70 mg cholesterol; 1338 mg sodium; 12.5 g carbohydrate; 3 g dietary fiber; 8.7 g total sugars; 21.1 g protein.

Mini Urfa Kebab

This kebab dish is not spicy, yet it is pleasing to your senses. The meat is kneaded along with the dill weed, parsley, hamburger bun, egg, cumin, paprika, garlic powder, black pepper and onion powder, making it more savory and flavorful. The meat mixture is shaped in a long and narrow tube and thread onto a wooden skewer.

Servings: 4 to 6

Ingredients

1 ½ pounds **ground 80% lean beef**

¼ cup chopped **dill weed**

1/3 cup chopped **Italian parsley leaves**

2 **plain hamburger** or **hot dog buns**

3 teaspoons **salt**

1 **egg**

1 tablespoon **sweet paprika**

2 tablespoons **garlic powder**

2 teaspoons **black pepper**

1 tablespoon **cumin powder**

2 tablespoons **onion powder**

25 pieces wooden skewers

Directions

Soak the wooden skewers in a large pan with water to prevent burning during cooking.

Wash the dill weed and parsley, shaking out excess water. Discard the stems. Finely chop the leaves and place them in a large mixing bowl of a stand mixer with a dough hook attachment.

Add the beef, hamburger or hot dog buns, salt, egg, sweet paprika, garlic powder, black pepper, and cumin powder.

Process the mixer on low until the ingredients are kneaded for twenty minutes, pushing the mixture to go back to the center for an even mixture.

If you are not using a stand mixer, knead the mixture manually using rubber gloves for twenty minutes.

When the consistency of the mixture is similar to dough, cover with plastic wrap and let rest in the fridge for 30 minutes.

Heat up the grill.

Equally divide the meat mixture into 25 portions.

Now is the time to thread the meat mixture by holding a skewer with your hand. Pick up 1 ball with the other hand. Open and close your hand and mold the meatball along the skewer to create a narrow, long tube and taper the ends to adhere to the stick.

Place the kebabs in rows on top of each other while waiting for the coals to burn down a little to evenly grill.

When using a gas grill, set it on high and then when cooking, reduce heat to medium.

Arrange the skewer slightly diagonal to the grill grate for nicely sear lines while touching the grill. Cover and cook for three to five minutes per side. Flip the kebabs with tongs to the opposite diagonal to cook the other side.

Garnish with fire roasted tomato wedges and hot green peppers.

Serve Urfa kebabs warm with bulgur wheat pilaf, rice pilaf or potatoes.

Serve!

Nutritional Information: 602 calorie; 32.4 g fat (11.7 g saturated fat); 192 mg cholesterol; 2050 mg sodium; 24.2 g carbohydrate; 3.3 g dietary fiber; 5.1 g total sugars; 52.3 g protein.

Turkish Vegetarian Meatballs With Red Lentils and Bulgur

Savor the taste of these delightful vegetarian meatballs cooked the Turkish way called 'mercimek köftesi. Boil the lentils along with seasonings, pepper, and bulgur and tomato paste. Knead the mixture along with lemon juice, green onions, parsley and olive oil.

Servings: 5-10

Ingredients

1 rounded cup **red lentils**

5 cups **water**

2 tablespoons **sweet red pepper paste**

2 tablespoons **tomato paste**

1/2 teaspoon **black pepper**

3 teaspoons **salt**

Pinch of **sugar**

1 1/2 cups **fine bulgur**

1 bunch of cleaned and chopped **green onions**

1 teaspoon **hot red pepper flakes**

1 large bunch of **Italian parsley**

1 teaspoon **lemon juice**

1 tablespoon **olive oil**

Directions

Wash the parsley, discard the thick stems and finely chop the leaves. Set aside.

Rinse the red lentils for several times in a fine mesh strainer until the water runs clear. Pour the lentils into a large saucepan and add enough water to cover. Bring to a boil on high heat.

When boiling, cover the pan with the lid cracked on low heat. Continue cooking until the lentils fall apart, adding more water if needed.

When there is too much liquid, drain it and if the water is too little, add boiled water to the lentils to bring to the right level which is about a half inch on top of the lentils.

Add the pepper paste, tomato and seasonings to lentils, stir to blend well.

Add the bulgur and stir until well blended. Cover the pan and let it cool down to allow the bulgur to absorb the extra water and soften naturally.

When the mixture is cool, knead it with lemon juice, olive oil, chopped parsley and green onions until incorporated; season with salt and pepper.

Prepare the serving plate and line it with lettuce leaves. Tear apart a large walnut size of the meat mixture and shape it into a long cylindrical shape with tapered ends.

Repeat with the rest of the meat mixture and arrange them on the serving platter on top of another. Garnish on top with chopped parsley leaves.

Serve!

Nutritional Information: 159 calorie; 2 g fat (0 g saturated fat); 0 mg cholesterol; 710 mg sodium; 30 g carbohydrate; 5 g dietary fiber; 8 g protein.

TURKISH WEDDING SOUP IS CALLED 'DÜĞÜN ÇORBASI'

This heirloom recipe has been handed down from the Ottoman era and up to these days; it is served at weddings and special events to celebrate a milestone. The düğün çorbasi is zesty and buttery and the preparation is a bit complex, yet the soup proves to be one of the best in Turkish cuisine.

Servings: 4

Ingredients

2 large **onions**

2 1/2 pounds **coarse chunks of lamb** or **mutton on the bone**

10 cups of **water**

3 heaping tablespoons **flour**

Juice of 2 lemons

3 **eggs**

1 teaspoon **dried basil**

3 tablespoons **butter**

1 teaspoon **tomato paste**

1 teaspoon **hot red pepper flakes**

Directions

Prepare the onions by removing the skin and place in a large covered saucepan.

Place the lamb chunks with bones on top of whole onions and cover with ten cups of water. Bring the lamb to a boil, covering the pan with lid cracked for ten to fifteen minutes.

Remove the foamy texture and blood that float on the surface of the liquid using a wire strainer. When the surface is clear, reduce the stove heat; cover and bring the meat to a gentle simmer for 1 ½ hours.

Remove the saucepan from heat when the meat falls away from the bones.

With a slotted spoon, remove the meat and bones and set aside. Let cool until easy to handle and discard the onions.

Discard the bones and separate the meat with your fingers into bite-sized pieces. Discard the bone fragments, fat and grizzle.

Strain the broth to totally remove any debris until you come up with 6 cups of broth.

Pour the broth into a clean saucepan and bring to a boil.

Meanwhile, combine the flour with a spoonful of water in a small bowl, stirring in with the broth to make a thin paste.

Add salt and drizzle in the boiling broth while stirring often.

Add the meat to the broth, and bring to a gentle simmer for twenty minutes longer.

Whisk in another bowl the egg yolks and lemon juice, and then whisk in a ladleful of hot broth and one more time.

Slowly sprinkle the mixture into the soup and at the same time stirring often.

Gently boil the soup for 1 minute and remove from heat.

Ladle the soup into individual bowls.

Melt in a small pan the butter and add the red pepper, basil and tomato paste.

Spoon the mixture over the top of the bowls with soup.

Serve!

Nutritional Information: 1050 calorie; 70 g fat (31 g saturated fat); 445 mg cholesterol; 646 mg sodium; 23 g carbohydrate; 3 g dietary fiber; 78 g protein.

Turkish Highland Meadow Soup (Yayla Çorbası)

This savory soup is favorable to your taste buds, even if it is your first time to try it. By looking at the ingredients, you can sense its creamy goodness with plain yogurt, egg yolk, and butter plus rice and spices. Each bowl is garnished with butter-mint mixture and mint leaves.

Servings: 2

Ingredients

1/2 cup **rice**

3 cups of **water**

2 cups **plain yogurt**

1 large **egg yolk**

1 cup **water**

2 tablespoons **all-purpose flour**

Dash **white pepper**

1 teaspoon **salt**

2 tablespoons **dried mint**

2 tablespoons **butter** or **margarine**

Optional:

1 teaspoon **hot red pepper flakes**

2 **fresh mint sprigs**

Directions

Rinse the rice and place in a covered saucepan. Add three cups of water; bring to a boil. Cover and simmer until the rice has softened.

Place in a separate bowl the egg, 1 cup of water, flour, and plain yogurt and beat briskly using a wire whisk until creamy and no single lump is present.

Gently whisk together the rice & water mixture with the yogurt & water mixture, and then add the white pepper and salt. Keep whisking while making sure that the soup does not reach boiling point.

Melt the butter in another pan and stir in the dried mint.

Stir often and remove the pan from heat and scrape into the soup while whisking until incorporated.

Ladle the soup into individual bowl and garnish with a sprig of fresh mint leaves.

Another option is to place the butter-mint mixture and drizzle over the soup. You can also add a teaspoon of hot red pepper flakes to the butter-mint mixture.

Serve!

Nutritional Information: 506 calorie; 17.4 g fat (10.7 g saturated fat); 150 mg cholesterol; 1435 mg sodium; 61.5 g carbohydrate; 1.5 g dietary fiber; 17.5 g total sugars; 19.8 g protein.

ADANA KEBAB (GROUND LAMB KEBAB)

This kebab uses ground lamb and mixed with garlic, onion, ground sumac, ground cumin, black pepper, salt, ice water and red pepper flakes. While grilling, a mixture of sumac and cumin is spread on top of kebab. Serve Adana Kebab with naan bread or warm pita bread.

Servings: 4

Ingredients

1 pound **ground lamb**

4 peeled and minced **cloves garlic**

1 peeled and minced small **onion**

1 1/2 teaspoons **ground sumac**, divided

1 1/2 teaspoons **ground cumin**, divided

1/4 teaspoon **ground black pepper**

1/2 teaspoon **salt**

2 tablespoons **ice cold water**

1/4 teaspoon **red pepper flakes**

4 pieces metal skewers or wooden skewers (soaked in water)

Directions

Mix in a large bowl, the ground lamb, garlic, onion, 1 teaspoon of ground cumin, 1 teaspoon ground sumac, ground black pepper, red pepper flakes, salt and ice water.

Using your hands, knead the mixture until tacky. Chill for thirty minutes.

Dip your fingers in water and thread a quarter of the lamb mixture onto the skewer.

When doing this use one ounce scoop to form the balls before threading onto the skewer and mash together.

Fire up your grill and cook the kebabs for 12 minutes until both sides are charred.

For the sauce, mix together the remaining sumac and ground cumin, and then sprinkle all over the kebabs during the grilling process.

Serve with naan bread or pita along with red onion and tomato slices, chopped parsley and diced cucumber.

Serve!

Nutritional Information: 226 calorie; 8.6 g fat (3 g saturated fat); 102 mg cholesterol; 380 mg sodium; 3.1 g carbohydrate; 0.8 g total sugars;0.6 g dietary fiber; 32.4 g protein.

TURKISH LIVER AND ONIONS RECIPE

Serve this authentic Turkish liver recipe using young, fresh lamb or calf liver. The tender texture starts during frying, which could only last for a few minutes unlike when you are using the liver of an older animal. It tastes so good and perfect for lunch and dinner.

Servings: 4

Ingredients

1 pound **fresh calf** or **lamb liver**

1 teaspoon **salt**

1 tsp. **black pepper**

6 tablespoons **flour**

1/2 teaspoon **paprika**

1/3 cup **olive oil** or **vegetable oil**

4 tablespoons **butter**

1 large **red onion**

1/3 cup **fresh Italian parsley**, chopped

1 teaspoon **ground sumac**

Directions

Dice the liver into cubes, about the size of dice and place in a colander. Rinse under cold running water to wash out extra blood. Let the liver drain in colander for a few minutes. When dried, place on paper towels to drain excess moisture.

Place in a Ziploc bag the salt, paprika, flour and pepper and shake to mix together.

Place the liver in the bag and shake until it is lightly covered with the mixture.

Melt in a large pan the oil and butter. Add the liver cubes and gently arrange in such a way that they are uniformly cooked in oil.

When browned, gently turn the raw side with a wooden spoon until both sides are browned, but not losing the flour.

Meanwhile, peel the onion, thinly slice and cut into quarters. Separate the onion rings and toss with salt, parsley and sumac.

To serve, line your plate with the onion mixture and spread on top with the cooked liver.

Serve with baked or fried potatoes.

Enjoy!

Nutritional Information: 704 calorie; 55 g fat (19 g saturated fat); 137 mg cholesterol; 1031 mg sodium; 21 g carbohydrate; 3 g dietary fiber; 31 g protein.

BEEF STEW OVER HOT, CREAMY EGGPLANT & CHEESE

This delicious Turkish dish is called 'Hunkar Beğendi' or 'the Sultan liked it,' in English. Perhaps the name is derived by its awesome taste due to the tender beef stew perched on hot creamy eggplant mash dotted with aged Turkish kaşar cheese. For sure the sultan or ordinary diner will love it to the max.

Servings: 6

Ingredients

1 grated **onion**

1 grated **tomato**

1 pound **top round beef**, cut into cubes

4 cups **fire-roasted eggplant** or **canned roasted eggplant**

3 rounded tablespoons **butter**

2 heaping tablespoons **flour**

3 to 4 cups **milk**

1 teaspoon **salt**

½ teaspoon **sugar**

½ teaspoon **pepper**

1/3 cup grated **aged Turkish kaşar cheese**

Freshly **ground white pepper**

1 teaspoon **salt**

Directions

Remove extra moisture from grated onion by squeezing.

Place onion in a covered saucepan with the grated tomatoes and beef. Season with sugar, salt and pepper and stir the ingredients to combine well.

Cook the mixture over high heat and simmer on low. Cover and gently simmer while stirring often, until the vegetables become tender and the mixture is thickened for one hour.

Prepare the eggplant mash by roasting and extracting the flesh of fresh eggplant.

If you are using preserved eggplant, drain and rinse in a fine wire strainer and press hard to remove extra moisture.

Melt in a shallow large pan the butter and stir in the flour for 1 or 2 minutes. Stir in milk with wire whisk to form into a smooth béchamel.

Add pepper, salt, and garlic (optional). Keep stirring with wire whisk on low heat, making sure it does not reach boiling point.

Stir in the cheese and eggplant, stir often until smooth and there are no more traces of eggplant.

Cover the pan and simmer on the lowest heat and let it bubble gently for 5 minutes. Stir and remove from heat.

Cover the bottom of serving platter with hot eggplant mash and arrange the piping hot beet stew in the center of the mash.

Sprinkle with a sprig of fresh rosemary.

Serve!

Nutritional Information: 397 calorie; 22.1 g fat (9.3 g saturated fat); 93 mg cholesterol; 1621 mg sodium; 16.1 g carbohydrate; 1.8 g dietary fiber; 6.9 g total sugars; 31 g protein.

Turkish-style Grilled Chicken with Yogurt and Cumin (Tavuk Izgara) Recipe

Dinner is getting exciting if you prepare some Turkish dishes that your family has never heard of. Like this grilled chicken thighs, marinated in Turkish style by pulsing the marinade consisting of toasted cumin seeds, garlic cloves, onion, paprika and lemon juice.

Servings: 4

Ingredients

2 tablespoons **toasted cumin seeds**

4 to 6 finely minced **garlic cloves**

1 small coarsely chopped **onion**

Juice of 1 lemon

1 tablespoon **paprika**

1 cup **plain yogurt**

12 **boneless chicken thighs** (about 2 to 2-1/2 pounds)

Pinch **salt**

Dash of freshly **ground black pepper**

Lemon wedges for serving

4 skewers

Directions

Toast in a small sauté pan the cumin seeds over medium heat until fragrant and popping in the pan. Remove from heat and grind.

Put together in a food processor the toasted cumin, garlic, onion, lemon juice and paprika. Pulse the ingredients until liquefied.

Add in the yogurt and pulse again until well blended.

Place the chicken thighs in a non-aluminum shallow baking dish and pour all over the marinade, tossing to coat well. Marinate for two hours at room temperature for two hours or chill overnight.

Build a charcoal fire by preheating the broiler.

Thread onto skewers the marinated chicken thighs and sprinkle with salt and pepper.

Grill or broil for six minutes per side until the liquid runs clear. Serve immediately with lemon wedges.

Enjoy!

Nutritional Information: 783 calorie; 41 g fat; 21 g carbohydrate; 80 g protein.

Homemade Turkish Tarhana

If you are planning to prepare a tarhana soup, it is important that you have a stock of the dry pulse that bears the same name, tarhana. The tarhana goes different stages of preparation from processing the veggies, fermentation, drying up and storing.

Ingredients

1 pound **tomatoes**

1 pound **onions**

1 pound **sweet red peppers**

4 cups of **water**

16 ounces **cooked or canned & drained chickpeas**

16 ounces **plain yogurt**

1 packet **active dry yeast**

1 teaspoon **hot red pepper flakes**

1 tablespoon **salt**

1 teaspoon **black pepper**

2 pounds **flour**

Directions

Rinse the vegetables and place in a large pot filled with water; bring to a gentle boil until very soft. Drain and add the precooked chickpeas.

Pour into a food processor and puree. Drain excess water by letting the pureed mixture sit in a fine wire strainer for several minutes.

When totally dry, pour into a large mixing bowl. Stir in yogurt until well blended.

Add the active dry yeast, hot red pepper flakes, salt and black pepper.

Slowly add the flour, working into the mixture with your gloved hands and do it several times until the batter is smooth.

Cover the bowl with cling wrap and then wrap the bowl with a towel. Let it stay in a warm place for five days, making sure to check and stir the batter every day if the fermentation process is even.

Remove the towel and cling wrap on the 5th day. Stir the mixture, which has a bright orange color and sour aroma.

Prepare the baking sheets by covering with non-stick baking parchment paper.

Divide the batter by filling the sheets with large spoonfuls of patties, and leave it in a dry place until the other side is totally dried up. Turn patties to dry up the other side.

When dried up, start breaking up the patties with your fingers. This is to completely dry the coarsely crumbled tarhana. Crumble and dry the rest of the patties until they become a fine powder.

Spread out on the sheets and let them dry by shifting them with your hands.

When the tarhana is totally dried and fine, store them in sealed glass containers for up to 1 year without refrigerating, so that you can use it in preparing soup.

To make a simple tarhana soup, all you have to do is to place a few spoonfuls of the pulse in a saucepan with water or hot milk and cook until thick. Season with salt, spices and add some butter.

Enjoy!

Nutritional Information: 53 calorie; 2 g fat (0 g saturated fat); 1 mg cholesterol; 207 mg sodium; 8 g carbohydrate; 1 g dietary fiber; 2 g protein.

Içli Köfte Recipe: A Turkish Stuffed Meatball

These içli köfte or stuffed meatball is a Turkish dish that you will fall in love with after tasting. The spicy filling is a blend of ground beef, walnuts, red pepper flakes, pepper, paprika, salt and onion. It is stuffed in a casing made of bulgur, potato, beef, egg and onion and fried in deep fat.

Servings: 24

Ingredients

For the filling:

1/4 pound **ground beef**

1 finely chopped small **onion**

1/3 cup **ground walnuts halves** or **shelled pistachios**

1/2 teaspoon **black pepper**

1/2 teaspoon **salt**

1/2 teaspoon **hot red pepper flakes**

1/2 teaspoon **paprika**

For the case:

1 tablespoon **ground beef**

1/3 cup **fine bulgur**

1/2 teaspoon **salt**

1/2 teaspoon **black pepper**

1/2 beaten **egg**

1/4 cup **mashed potato**

1 grated small **onion**

3 to 4 cups **sunflower oil** for frying

Fresh Italian parsley

Directions
Make the filling:

Fry in a small skillet the ¼ pound ground beef until cooked.

Stir in onion until softened. Stir in ground nuts, black pepper, salt, hot red pepper flakes, and paprika. Stir often until the flavors are well combined. Remove from heat and let meat mixture rest.

Make the case:

Combine in a large mixing bowl the 1 tablespoon ground beef with bulgur, black pepper, egg, salt, onion and potato.

Wearing a pair of gloves, knead together the mixture several times to form dough.

Tear apart pieces of dough about the size of walnut and shape into balls, pushing some of the nut and meat filling towards the center of the dough and seal the end.

Form the meatballs into football shape or spindle by making the ends, narrow and the middle part, thicker.

Pour 3 to 4 cups of sunflower oil in a large skillet and heat over medium high.

Fry the meatballs in hot oil until the sides are evenly dark golden brown; drain on paper towels.

Garnish stuffed meatballs with fresh Italian parsley.

Serve it piping hot with dipping sauce made of plain yogurt, fresh dill and grated cucumber.

Enjoy!

Nutritional Information: 1001 calorie; 111 g fat (11 g saturated fat); 10 mg cholesterol; 8 mg sodium; 3 g carbohydrate; 1 g dietary fiber; 2 g protein.

Tavuk Sış: Authentic Turkish Chicken Kebab

Your family dinner would turn into an exciting moment with this authentic Turkish chicken kebab or tavuk siş. The chicken is soaked in a marinade composed of plain yogurt, garlic & onion juices, tomato paste, paprika, oil, pepper and salt that makes the kebab juicy, succulent and aromatic.

Servings: 6 to 8 kebabs

Ingredients

2 **boneless &skinless chicken breasts** or 4 to 5 boneless & skinless thighs

2 **cloves garlic**

1 medium **onion**

3 tablespoons **vegetable oil**

1/2 cup **plain yogurt** or **milk**

1 teaspoon **ground black pepper**

2 tablespoons **tomato paste**

1 teaspoon **salt**

1 teaspoon **paprika**

Garnish:

Oregano

Sumac

Paprika

6 to 8 bamboo or wooden skewers

Directions

Heat up a grill to medium.

Wash the chicken breast several times under cold running water and blot dry on paper towels.

Cut the breasts into bite-sized cubes as big as a large dice.

Grate the garlic cloves and onion using a fine grate to produce a pulp and pour into a very fine mesh strainer. Press the juice out into a separate bowl, using a wooden spoon; discard the garlic and onion pulp.

Combine in a large glass bowl the garlic & onion juices, tomato paste, yogurt or milk, oil, paprika, pepper and salt. Toss the cubed chicken into the mixture to coat well. Cover and chill for four hours or overnight.

Soak the bamboo skewers in water for several hours to prevent burning on the grill. Remove chicken pieces from marinade.

Thread five chicken pieces onto the bamboo or metal skewer, making sure they are not too close so they are evenly cooked. Sprinkle with salt before placing the kebabs on the hot grill.

Grill for twelve minutes, turning once in a while to evenly cook.

For added flavor, sprinkle hot kebabs with sumac, paprika and oregano.

Serve kebabs with your favorite rice pilaf or veggie and bulgur salad or bread.

Enjoy!

Nutritional Information: 394 calorie; 23 g fat (6 g saturated fat); 107 mg cholesterol; 113 mg sodium; 10 g carbohydrate; 1 g dietary fiber; 35 g protein.

TURKISH 'LADY'S THIGH MEATBALLS

These hearty köfte or meatballs are enough to satiate your hunger. Each meatball is packed with cooked rice, egg, ground beef, fresh dill, allspice and pepper. The kneaded mixture is dredged on flour and dip in beaten egg before cooking in deep fat.

Servings: 2

Ingredients

1/2 cup **cooked white rice; cooked plain rice** or **leftover rice pilaf**

1/2 pound **ground 85-90% fat beef**

1 **egg**

2 teaspoons **salt**

1/2 cup chopped **fresh dill**

2 teaspoons **ground allspice**

1/2 teaspoons **black pepper**

1 cup **flour**

2 beaten **eggs**

2 cups **vegetable oil** for deep frying

Directions

Combine the ground beef, egg, cooked rice, salt, black pepper, ground allspice and fresh dill and knead for several minutes until incorporated. Let mixture rest for a few minutes.

Break off large meat mixture pieces to create flat oblong and plump meatballs that can be fitted in your palms.

Evenly spread the flour on a large plate and roll the meatballs to coat evenly.

Beat in a bowl the eggs; season with salt.

Tap the meatballs to remove excess flour and dip in the beaten egg until thoroughly coated.

Place the meatballs in hot oil and fry until golden brown. Repeat these steps with the rest of the meatballs, flour, and egg.

Flip the meatballs over using a strainer to cook both sides equally.

Drain fried meatballs on paper towels. Serve with mac & cheese, French fries, or rice pilaf.

Enjoy!

Nutritional Information: 651 calorie; 20.5 g fat (4.9 g saturated fat); 100 mg cholesterol; 2436 mg sodium; 93.5 g carbohydrate; 4.5 g dietary fiber; 0.6 g total sugars; 24 g protein.

Köfte: Turkish Grilled Meatballs

These grilled meat patties called köfte is a perfect combination of ground beef, stale white bread, Italian parsley and seasonings. After a quick kneading, the patties are grilled. You can also form the meatballs into cylindrical, oblong, round or patty and you can grill, broil, bake, pan-fry, or stew.

Servings: 4

Ingredients

1 pound **ground 80% to 85% lean beef**

1 grated **small onion**

1 to 2 finely chopped **garlic cloves** or 1 teaspoon **garlic powder**

1 **egg**

2 teaspoons **salt**

1/4 cup chopped **fresh Italian parsley**

Black pepper to taste

3 slices **stale white bread** or 1/3 cup **plain breadcrumbs**

Directions

Heat up your grill to medium.

Mix in a large mixing bowl, the ground beef, egg, onion, garlic cloves, Italian parsley, salt and black pepper.

Remove the crusts of stale white bread and sprinkle with water, squeezing out to remove excess liquid. Add the wet bread to the mixture.

Quickly knead the ingredients for several times until incorporated and let rest.

Remove an apricot-sized piece from the meat mixture and form into balls.

Flatten with the palm of your hands to look like patties. Grill the patty, flipping once, until both sides are evenly browned.

Serve!

Nutritional Information: 126 calorie; 4.8 g fat (1.7 g saturated fat); 59 mg cholesterol; 1326 mg sodium; 12 g carbohydrate; 1 g dietary fiber; 1.7 g total sugars; 8.5 g protein.

BEEF SHISH KEBAB RECIPE

The beef is marinated in a mixture of white vinegar, olive oil, coriander, cumin, garlic, and paprika for several hours. The beef cubes are then threaded onto skewers while the optional vegetables are threaded separately and grilled.

Servings: 8 servings beef shish kebab

Ingredients

2 pounds **beef sirloin** or **tenderloin**, cut into 1-inch cubes

1 tablespoon **white vinegar**

1/2 cup **olive oil**

1/2 teaspoon **coriander**

1 teaspoon **cumin**

1 teaspoon minced **garlic**

1/2 teaspoon **paprika**

Optional:

Bell peppers

Wedges of **red onion**

Mushrooms

Directions

Combine in a freezer bag the olive oil, vinegar, coriander, cumin, garlic, beef cubes, and paprika. Shake until well blended.

Place the beef in the freezer bag, shake and refrigerate for several hours until ready to grill.

Remove the beef from the marinade and thread the meat pieces onto skewers soaked in water.

Thread the optional vegetables onto separate skewers as they cook more quickly than the beef.

Heat up the grill on medium and spray with cooking oil.

Place the beef and grill for five to seven minutes per side until done.

Serve kebabs with rice pilaf, grilled veggies or pita bread.

Enjoy!

Nutritional Information: 314 calorie; 20 g fat (4 g saturated fat); 95 mg cholesterol; 70 mg sodium; 0 g carbohydrate; 0 g dietary fiber; 32 g protein.

Beyti Kebab Recipe

This Turkish kebab will surely tickle your gustatory taste with all the flavors and blended together to come up with a spicy, saucy, creamy and savory dish. The meat mixture is grilled and rolled in tortilla wraps and served with tomato sauce and rice pilaf.

Servings: 4

Ingredients

1 ½ tablespoons **bread crumbs from white bread**

1.2 pounds chopped **lamb**

½ tablespoon **milk**

½ teaspoon **red chili pepper**

2 teaspoons **cracked coriander**

2 teaspoons **bumped cumin**

2 chopped **tomatoes**

2 tablespoons **tomato paste**

1 tablespoon **olive oil**

1 teaspoon **garlic powder**

4 tablespoons **plain yogurt**

1 teaspoon **onion powder**

Pinch of **salt**

Dash **pepper**

4 to 5 **tortillas**

Directions

Soak the breadcrumbs in the milk for a few minutes.

Mix in a large bowl the bread crumbs, cumin, lamb, coriander, chili pepper, ½ teaspoon freshly squeezed pepper, and salt. Chill for 1 hour.

Grill the mixture over hot charcoal on a wide skewer for twenty minutes, flipping to cook the other side.

Meanwhile, heat the oil in a skillet on medium heat and add the chopped tomatoes, tomato puree, onion powder, garlic powder, pepper and salt. Bring tomato sauce to a boil.

Roll the grilled meat mixture into the tortilla wraps; bake the ends.

Cut the Beyti kebab into bite-sized pieces. Serve with tomato sauce, yogurt and rice pilaf.

Enjoy!

Nutritional Information: 397 calorie;15.1 g fat (4.5 g saturated fat); 124 mg cholesterol; 199 mg sodium; 21.8 g carbohydrate; 3.3 g dietary fiber; 4.6 g total sugars; 42.5 g protein.

PATLICANLI KEBABI

Patlicanli Kebabı or eggplant kebab is originally cooked on wood fire by threading the meatballs and eggplants in skewers. In this recipe, the eggplant kebab is cooked in the oven as the easiest way to prepare them, but it does not make a difference. It is still delicious, juicy and flavorful.

Servings: 4

Ingredients

4 **eggplants**

½ pound **ground beef**

1 grated big **onion**

1 teaspoon **black pepper**

1/4 cups **bread crumbs**

1 teaspoon **cumin**

2 teaspoons **salt**

4 tablespoons **olive oil**

2 **tomatoes**, cut into halve

4 **green peppers**

Directions

Prepare the eggplants by slicing into circular shape, but not too thin. Soak in salted water for fifteen minutes, set aside.

Prepare the meatballs by combining the ground meat, bread crumbs, grated onion, black pepper, cumin and salt.

Knead the meat mixture for several minutes and take a walnut-sized piece and roll them in your hand and flatten out by pressing with your palms. Repeat this step for the rest of the meat mixture.

Preheat the oven at 356 degrees F.

Coat an oven tray with oil.

Drain the eggplants and lay on the tray together with the meatballs. Do this by placing the meatballs in between the eggplant slices to form a whole eggplant, and then do the rest of the meatballs and eggplant slices.

Place the tomato halves in the tray together with the green peppers.

Drizzle 4 tablespoons of olive oil over the vegetables and meatballs. Bake for 45 minutes. Check the eggplants if they are already soft by pricking with a fork and if they are still hard, continue cooking for five to ten minutes.

Arrange the eggplant & meatball combination on a serving plate.

Place the tomato slices and peppers beside the eggplant kebab, so they can stand still.

Serve piping hot.

Enjoy!

Nutritional Information: 438 calorie; 19.4 g fat (3.5 g saturated fat); 51 mg cholesterol; 1269 mg sodium; 48.1 g carbohydrate; 23.2 g dietary fiber; 22.5 g total sugars; 25.5 g protein.

ÇÖP ŞİŞ (KEBAB ON A STICK)

This popular grilled dish called çöp şiş are simply irresistible. The kebab on a stick is not only ideal treat for dinner, but it is recommended for potluck, camping and picnicking with the thrill of cooking them outdoors. You can grill the kebab over wood fire, electric grill or pan grill.

Servings: 4

Ingredients

1-1.7 pounds **cubed lamb**

5 tablespoons **milk**

4 tablespoons **olive oil**

1 tablespoon **fresh lemon juice**

½ tablespoon **brown sugar**

½ tablespoon **soy sauce**

½ tablespoon **honey**

2 crushed **cloves garlic**

1 teaspoon **sea salt**

½ roughly chopped medium-sized **onion**

½ **red pepper flakes**

½ teaspoon **ground red sweet pepper**

½ tablespoon **mustard sauce**

1/4 teaspoon **black pepper ground**

1 tablespoon **fresh thyme**

4 leaves **fresh mint**

1 tablespoon **fresh basil leaves**

1 tablespoon **fresh rosemary**

Garniture:

10 to 15 **cherry tomatoes**

3 to 4 fresh sliced **green pepper**

10 to 20 wooden skewers

Directions

Soak the wooden skewers in water for 2 to 3 minutes, set aside.

Combine in a bowl the milk, olive oil, brown sugar, soy sauce, honey, garlic, lemon juice, sea salt, onion, ground red pepper, black pepper, mustard and red pepper flakes.

Add the herbs to the mixture and mix together until well incorporated.

Pour marinade over the cubed lamb, tossing to coat well. Cover the bowl with plastic wrap and refrigerate for two to four hours or overnight for best results.

When ready to grill, remove the bowl from the fridge and let it stay at room temperature for half an hour.

Thread the marinated lamb, tomato and fresh pepper onto wooden skewers and cook on griddle pan or electric grill for six to eight minutes until golden brown and thoroughly cooked.

Serve!

Nutritional Information: 663 calorie; 33 g fat (8.1 g saturated fat); 175 mg cholesterol; 794 mg sodium; 33.7 g carbohydrate; 9 g dietary fiber; 20.6 g total sugars; 60.6 g protein.

Homemade Doner Kebab: A Turkish Classic

This awesome Turkish sandwich version is enough to make your stomach full with yummy baked lamb loaf stuffed into the pita bread and piled with lettuce, tomato, cucumber, red onion and then drizzled with tahini or Tsatziki sauce.

Servings: 4

Ingredients

For the Kebab:

1 pound **ground lamb** or a **combination of half ground beef and half ground lamb**

4 peeled and finely minced **cloves garlic**

1 teaspoon **smoked paprika**

1 **egg**

1 teaspoon **ground coriander**

1/4 teaspoon **ground black pepper**

1 teaspoon **ground cumin**

1/2 teaspoon **salt**

1 teaspoon **dried oregano**

For the Sandwich:

4 pieces rounds of **pita** or **naan** or **flatbread**

1 cup **assorted lettuce**

1 sliced large **tomato**

1/2 sliced seedless **English cucumber**

1/4 peeled and sliced large **red onion**

Tsatziki sauce or **tahini sauce**

Directions

Preheat the oven at 350 degree Fahrenheit.

Combine in a large mixing bowl, the ground lamb, garlic, egg, ground cumin, smoked paprika, ground coriander, dried oregano, black pepper and salt. Transfer the meat mixture into a loaf pan.

Bake for thirty minutes until the surface is nicely golden brown.

Slice the loaf after cooling completely or wrap the doner kebab in aluminum foil and chill until firm for best results.

When reheating, heat a little olive oil in a large pan and cut the loaf into very thin slices, and then reheat for a few minutes.

Assemble the sandwich by piling the kebab and the vegetables.

Slather with Tsatziki or tahini sauce.

Serve!

Nutritional Information: 423 calorie; 18.2 g fat (4.4 g saturated fat); 143 mg cholesterol; 683 mg sodium; 24 g carbohydrate; 3.2 g dietary fiber; 2.9 g total sugars; 39 g protein.

CONCLUSION

Thank you so much for downloading this Book. We at Savour Press hope this book has increased your knowledge regarding some original and authentic Turkish recipes. This eBook contains a curated list of what we believe to be the 10 best Turkish side dishes and 33 best Turkish main dishes which cover a variety of flavors and tastes. All different categories of Turkish dishes are represented such as your salads, meatballs, casseroles, kebabs, soups, rice pilaf, stew, and many more. During the making of this cookbook, our team decided that the recipes should be easy to understand by adding some descriptions of certain ingredients, so you will have an idea how the recipes are prepared and how they actually look like. Although some ingredients may sound alien to you, they can be bought in imported goods in supermarkets. When you are ready to try the recipes, you know how to get started. This book provides answers to your search for the best recipes for your loved ones, friends and guests.

We hope you will enjoy cooking with these recipes.

Thanks again for your support.

Happy Cooking!